A Walking Map of Dylan Thomas' New York

1. Hotel Chelsea
2. St. Vincent's Hospital
3. Patchin Place
4. Jefferson Market Courthouse
5. Julius' Bar
6. Hotel Earle
7. Washington Square
8. Grand Ticino Restaurant
9. Minetta Tavern
10. White Horse Tavern

WEST 23rd ST.

SEVENTH AVE.

EIGHTH AVE.

1

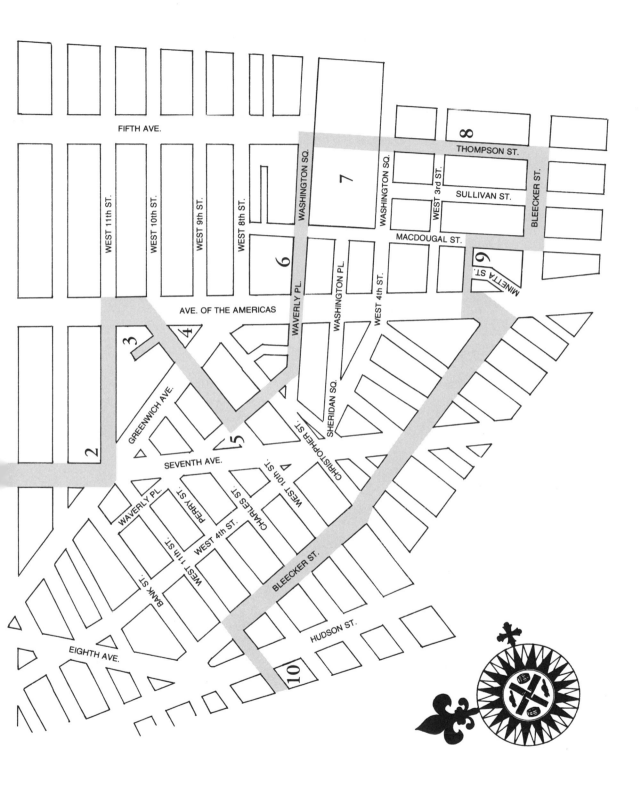

FIFTH AVE.

WEST 11th ST.

WEST 10th ST.

WEST 9th ST.

WEST 8th ST.

WASHINGTON SQ.

7

WASHINGTON SQ.

THOMPSON ST.

8

WEST 3rd ST.

SULLIVAN ST.

BLEECKER ST.

MACDOUGAL ST.

6

WAVERLY PL.

WASHINGTON PL.

WEST 4th ST.

9

MINETTA ST.

AVE. OF THE AMERICAS

3

4

GREENWICH AVE.

SHERIDAN SQ.

CHRISTOPHER ST.

2

5

SEVENTH AVE.

WAVERLY PL.

PERRY ST.

CHARLES ST.

WEST 10th ST.

WEST 11th ST.

WEST 4th ST.

BANK ST.

BLEECKER ST.

HUDSON ST.

EIGHTH AVE.

10

DYLAN THOMAS'
NEW YORK

''*One:* I am a Welshman;

Two: I am a drunkard;

Three: I am a lover of the human race,

especially of women.''

DYLAN THOMAS

NEW YORK

by Tryntje Van Ness Seymour

Stemmer
House
PUBLISHERS, INC.

Owings Mills, Maryland, 1978

Published simultaneously in Canada by George J. McLeod, Limited, Toronto

Excerpts from Dylan Thomas, *Under Milk Wood,* copyright © 1954 by
New Directions Publishing Corporation, reprinted by permission of
New Directions Publishing Corporation.
Quotations from John Malcolm Brinnin, *Dylan Thomas in America,* copyright
© 1955 by John Malcolm Brinnin, reprinted by permission of Little, Brown
and Company in association with Atlantic Monthly Press

This paperbound edition is based on a collector's limited edition clothbound
in a larger format published by Lime Rock Press, Inc., of Salisbury, Connecticut
06068.

A Barbara Holdridge book
Printed and bound in the United States of America
First paperbound edition

Library of Congress Cataloging in Publication Data
Seymour, Tryntje Van Ness.
    Dylan Thomas' New York.

    Text and photos by T. Van Ness Seymour accompanied by selections from
D. Thomas' Under milk wood.
    1.   Thomas, Dylan, 1914–1953—Homes and haunts—New York (City)—
Addresses, essays, lectures.   2.   Poets, Welsh—20th century—Biography—
Addresses, essays, lectures.   3.   Large type books.   4.   New York (City)—
Description—1951–   —Addresses, essays, lectures.   I.   Thomas, Dylan,
1914–1953. Under milk wood. Selections. 1978.   II.   Title.
PR6039.H52Z8486   1978   821'.9'12   78-13286
ISBN 0-916144-32-1

"A haven cosy as toast,
cool as an icebox,
and safe as skyscrapers."

"I love Third Avenue.

don't believe New York.

It's obvious to anyone why.

All the same, I believe in New Yorkers. Whether they've ever questioned the dream in which they live, I wouldn't know, because I won't ever dare ask that question.''

The date was

October 25, 1953.

The place, New York City.
The event, a full cast perform
a ''play for voices'' by Dylan

The final lines had just been
''A thousand people were left
and its grandeur,'' wrote John

The poet himself was delight
The performance was just as
He beamed.

Two weeks later he was dead.

nce of *Under Milk Wood,*
Thomas.

poken.
hushed by its lyrical harmonies
Malcolm Brinnin.

d. At last the play was right.
Thomas had planned it.

Dylan Thomas—considered by many the finest poet of the twentieth century—was born almost exactly 39 years before, on October 27, 1914, in Swansea, a small fishing village in South Wales. There he received all the formal education he would have, at the Swansea Grammar School, where he first started writing his poetry at age 11 and where several of his poems appeared in the *Swansea Grammar School Magazine.* During the four years following grammar school, between his sixteenth and twentieth birthdays, Thomas wrote about 200 poems—four times as many as he would write during the remaining nineteen years of his life. Between 1931 and 1932 he also worked as proofreader and apprentice reporter for the *South Wales Daily Post.* Then, for the next two years, he was involved in amateur acting with the Swansea Little Theatre.

Thomas' first book, *Eighteen Poems,* was published when he was only twenty years old. His second, *Twenty-five Poems,* was published two years later, in 1936. The following year he married Caitlin Macnamara at Penzance, Cornwall. He continued to work on his poetry, and in 1939 and 1940 published *The Map of Love, The World I Breathe,* and *Portrait of the Artist as a Young Dog.* In 1940 he was rejected for military service and moved to London where, for the next four years, he worked on scenarios for documentary films. Between 1945 and 1949 Thomas did frequent broadcasts for B.B.C., published *Deaths and Entrances,* and wrote three scripts for feature-length films (*Rebecca's Daughters, The Beach of Falesa,* and *Me and My Bike*—a film operetta), none of which were put into production at that time. In 1949 his third child was born and he moved to the Boat House, Laugharne, which was to be his home for the balance of his life.

During the next four years, Dylan Thomas made four visits to America at the invitation of John Malcolm Brinnin, Director of the Poetry Center at the Young Men's and Young Women's Hebrew Association in New York City. Thomas' first visit was between February 21 and May 31, 1950, during which time he gave readings at the Poetry Center and at a number of American colleges. In that same year he published *Twenty-six Poems.*

He made his second visit to America between January 20 and May 16, 1952, following a schedule similar to his first visit. He also published *In Country Sleep* and his *Collected Poems*—a collection of eighty-nine poems which he considered all he wished preserved at that time.

In 1953, Thomas made his third and fourth visits to America, from April 21 to June 3, and again from October 19 until his death on November 9. During these last two visits, in addition to his readings of poetry selections, Thomas gave readings and performances of *Under Milk Wood*.

On all of his trips to America, New York City served as Thomas' base for the lecture tours he made of college campuses and for his other out-of-town poetry readings. Dylan Thomas' principal public forum in New York itself was the Kaufmann Auditorium of the YM-YWHA at 92nd Street and Lexington Avenue.

John Brinnin served as the poet's manager, advisor and Boswell during much of the time he was here. Brinnin later produced a comprehensive—if depressing—chronicle of Dylan Thomas' travels, exploits and decline, *Dylan Thomas in America,* which is the basic source book for anyone interested in the full details of these visits.

Dylan Thomas' haunts in New York were limited to three sections of the city: Third Avenue; Chelsea; and Greenwich Village. For better or worse, the Third Avenue section Dylan Thomas knew in the early 1950s has been obliterated. With that constant penchant the City has for tearing down and rebuilding itself, the colorful Irish bars of post-World War II New York are gone, replaced by faceless office buildings with neither souls nor character. One of Thomas' favorite hangouts, Costello's, has moved to a new location on East 44th Street. The management has made some effort to recreate the old atmosphere, but the spirit is gone.

In Chelsea and Greenwich Village, however, the story is quite different. Although a quarter-century has taken its toll, and several of Thomas' pubs have disappeared, the core elements are still there. The special mood of those neighboring sections of the city still remains as it was when Dylan Thomas found a sympathetic home there during his visits. Happily, many of the landmarks associated with Thomas' sojourns are also still standing and in full operation—two of them, the Hotel Chelsea and the White Horse Tavern, in "mint" condition.

One can walk the streets in these parts of town today and see the same sights Dylan Thomas saw. Smell the same smells. Sense the same sensitivity to the value of the individual and the worth of freedom that has attracted so many kindred spirits of every size, shape and age.

Greenwich Village in particular is still home to the creative artist and dissenter, as it has been since the days of Thomas Paine, Herman Melville, Edgar Allan Poe, Samuel Clemens, Edna St. Vincent Millay, Willa Cather, and so many others. There is a chemistry at work in the Village, an interaction of different elements, which cannot be precisely identified or defined, and which has never been exactly duplicated elsewhere. Dylan Thomas became part of this chemical process during the last four years of his life.

On his first day in New York, February 21, 1950, Dylan Thomas was taken to Greenwich Village by his host, John Brinnin, and introduced to the sites which Thomas would frequent during the next few years. They visited Julius' bar on West 10th Street and Waverly Place, walked across Washington Square, had dinner at the Grand Ticino on Thompson Street, and then went to the San Remo bar at Bleecker and Macdougal Streets.

The San Remo has since closed, although the premises are still there. The other three places, however, are still very much in evidence.

Julius' is a corner bar decorated with photos of boxers and racehorses, a World War I helmet, and festoons of black, sticky dust on ceilings and walls. It was a favorite Village pub for many years following Prohibition up through the time of Thomas' visit. In recent years it has become a homosexual hangout and casual family trade is not encouraged. But the decor remains the same and a passing look through the open door or a plate glass window still reveals the setting as Thomas saw it in February, 1950.

The Grand Ticino is one of the finest of the family-style Italian restaurants in the Village. Anyone interested in Dylan Thomas or in New York would be well rewarded by its authentic white-table-clothed atmosphere, old-world hospitality, and excellent kitchen.

Washington Square continues to be a focal point of Village life. Although it has since undergone a face-lifting with new lighting and furnishings, the basic flavor of the park is still as it was when Henry James and, later, Eleanor Roosevelt lived on its north and west sides. Musicians, lovers, old folks, toddlers, protesters, bums, students—and poets— all are welcome here. With rare exceptions they treat each other, and visitors, with tolerance and mutual respect.

After Dylan Thomas visited Washington Square on that first day, he soon was living right next door, in the Hotel Earle on Waverly Place, just a few yards west of the park.

The Earle was a threadbare hostelry in the 1950s, with a devil-may-care air. It has since fallen on hard times and has been through the ordeal of serving as temporary shelter for down-and-out families on public welfare. When the author visited the hotel while researching this book, an inquiry of the management as to what room had been occupied by Dylan Thomas brought only a blank stare. They had never heard of him.

Dylan Thomas composed a letter to his parents in May 1950 from his bedroom at the Hotel Earle, which he described as being "right in Washington Square, a beautiful Square, which is right in the middle of Greenwich Village, the artists' quarter of New York."

Other Village institutions which became part of Dylan Thomas' life in New York included Minetta Tavern, a few blocks south on Macdougal Street. The tavern, although "renovated," still flourishes as a lively neighborhood saloon. It was then headquarters for a bearded Village character named Joe Gould, who spent his days riding the subways composing his monumental *Oral History of Our Time* on miscellaneous scraps of paper, and his evenings cadging drinks from patrons who came to hear his lively recitations about anything and everything. The Tavern was just a few doors north of San Remo, which served for a time as another Dylan Thomas favorite, where Maxwell Bodenheim regularly sold typewritten copies of his own poems for a dollar each to finance his own thirst-quenching.

Soon after his arrival, Dylan Thomas paid a visit to another Village institution, Patchin Place, just behind the Jefferson Market Courthouse at 10th Street and the Avenue of the Americas. Here lived and worked the poet e.e. cummings and his wife, Marion Morehouse. Brinnin, who had arranged the appointment, was present. He described the meeting of the two well-known poets as intimately sympathetic. "As our teatime conversation ranged lightly over literary terrain, it seemed to me that some of their judgments showed the acerb, profound and confident insights of artists who in their work have defined a world within the world, and that some showed merely the conspiratorial naughtiness of gleefully clever schoolboys."

The two great Dylan Thomas landmarks in New York, however—well worth a visit by anyone who savors the personalities of places and things—are the Hotel Chelsea and the White Horse Tavern. The Chelsea is located on West 23rd Street, between Seventh and Eighth Avenues. The White Horse Tavern is at the corner of West 11th and Hudson Streets.

Dylan Thomas brought his wife Caitlin with him on his second visit to New York in June 1952. They searched for an apartment with a kitchenette, and happily discovered the Hotel Chelsea, which just filled the bill. The Chelsea, constructed in 1883, is a solid mass of masonry and cast iron, reminiscent of the Left Bank in Paris. The two main architectural features of particular note are the balconies extending across the front of the building, and the brass-railed stairwell in the center of the structure, running from the huge skylight to just above the lobby level. Fire laws have forced the blocking off of the lobby so that one is denied a straight view up the center of the stairwell, but other views from the landings are striking.

The hotel also has an open roof area, accessible by staircase from the top floor, which gives a good view of wide sweeps of Manhattan and the blocks of row houses to the south. Several roof-top apartments are visible, with angled roofs and windows, which give them an odd, urbanized fairytale appearance. Other literary figures have found themselves at home at the Chelsea, including Thomas Wolfe, O. Henry, and Arthur Miller.

Creative artists in other fields, such as Sarah Bernhardt, John Sloan, Larry Rivers, Jackson Pollock and Virgil Thompson, also have lived there. It is both an artistic and architectural landmark of New York, marred only by tasteless modernization of the entrance and lobby area.

The Hotel Chelsea became Dylan Thomas' New York home from the first moment of discovery on his 1952 visit. He stayed there when he returned for the first New York performances of *Under Milk Wood* in the spring of 1953, and for the revisions in October 1953. It was at the Chelsea that much of the final writing on the work took place.

It was also at the Hotel Chelsea that Dylan Thomas' battle with himself and his self-doubts reached its final climax, and it was from there that he was taken unconscious by ambulance to St. Vincent's Hospital to die, after lingering in a coma for several days.

St. Vincent's is straight up 11th Street from the White Horse Tavern. "The Horse," as Dylan Thomas affectionately called it, was the scene of hundreds of happy hours spent by the poet in the familiar setting of an English pub and the comfortable surroundings of friends and well-wishers. It was a regular stop for him when he was in the city, and he spent hours on end there enjoying everything about the place.

As well he might. For the White Horse Tavern was and is an old-style neighborhood bar at its best. The bar has an array of regular patrons from the surrounding blocks, many of them longshoremen and truck drivers. Blue-collar workers and bearded writers rub elbows together easily at the White Horse. Any perceptive visitor feels at home immediately in the friendly, easy-going atmosphere.

The White Horse Tavern occupies the ground floor of a 3-story brick-and-frame corner building. There are two rooms, both with pressed-tin ceilings. The smaller room consists entirely of wooden tables and chairs, jammed in together helter-skelter, where patrons often pass the hours with a game of chess. Adjoining is the larger front room, with a dark wooden bar running its length in front of the mirror, then making an L-shaped turn at the right end, where a small short-order open kitchen turns out the limited food items on the menu.

All is dark brown, accented by bright neon beer advertising signs. A plaster sculpture of a horse—long since yellowed with age and dust—stands in one of the front windows. A large red neon sign with a blue horse's head hangs above the entrance and serves as a friendly beacon for passers-by along Hudson Street.

Draft beer in glass mugs is the staple at the White Horse, but anything else can be obtained on request. Dylan Thomas usually drank Scotch whisky. When Thomas returned to New York aboard the S.S. United States on April 21, 1953, the first place he went was the Hotel Chelsea, and one of the next was the White Horse Tavern. Brinnin described the joyful reunion:

"At the White Horse Tavern, which we reached by mid-afternoon, everyone along the bar turned to greet him. Ernie, the rotund proprietor, sent Scotch to our table and sat down with us to reminisce about memorable evenings of the year before. Dylan seemed happy, more than a little excited and, most of all, at home. His only genuine ease, I had long before observed, was among friendly faces, known or unknown, in places where the only propriety was to be oneself."

The last place Dylan Thomas visited just prior to his death was also the White Horse Tavern. He had two beers, chatted with a truck driver, then went back to the Hotel Chelsea, delirium tremens, and the ambulance.

The stark tragedy and waste of Dylan Thomas' death was not the result of this environment, but rather of the responsibilities of the larger world, with which he could not cope alone. Brinnin's analysis was blunt:

"Dylan drank primarily in defense, out of a need for a barrier between his guilt and his laughter, between himself and the world around him, even between himself and one other person. When he felt this need—and I had begun to understand by now that his coming to America had been undertaken in nothing short of terror—intoxication was a kind of license by which he was able to participate in, and at the same time keep himself responsibly removed from, situations he could not control."

Brinnin pointed out that Thomas' poems were always written when he was sober, when "his genius was his whole stimulant." Alcohol was related to something else.

"His drinking was not a means of denying or fleeing life," wrote Brinnin, "not a way of making it tolerable, but of fiercely embracing it."

Dylan Thomas had plans to do a series of major works at the time of his death in 1953. He had committed himself to a collaboration with Stravinsky which had not even begun. He had other large ideas in formulation. The one opus he was able to complete was *Under Milk Wood,* which he finished less than a month before he died.

Under Milk Wood is an insider's view of a day's activities in a small seacoast village in Wales. It is an expanded and more fully developed version of his earlier short prose piece, *Quite Early One Morning,* written in 1945. His work on the play extended over a number of years, but the final writing and polishing took place in Cambridge, Massachusetts and in New York City, much of it at the Hotel Chelsea.

The first public reading of the play was at the Fogg Museum in Cambridge on Sunday, May 3, 1953. Dylan Thomas had been living in Cambridge the previous week working almost solidly on the play. On the day of the reading he worked on revisions and additions from late morning until late afternoon. Finally he performed the still unfinished play as a solo piece. As Brinnin described the evening, "The play proceeded in an atmosphere of crackling excitement from its first solemn moments to its later passages of zany comedy and its final mellow embrace of a whole village of the living and the dead."

The first performance of the play with a full cast of actors was to take place two weeks later in the Kaufmann Auditorium of the YM-YWHA. During the interval Thomas continued to work on the play, mostly in the Hotel Chelsea, but, as time pressed, anywhere that he had a chance to write, including trains and planes to and from out-of town poetry readings. His room at the Chelsea was strewn with bits and pieces of paper with new lines to the play on them. The day of the first full performance Thomas was still writing. With breaks for rehearsals he worked steadily with two typists. The last third of the play was still unorganized and only partially written. However, in order to keep from having the performance cancelled at the last minute he made one final effort and was able to devise a tentative conclusion that could be used.

Shortly before curtain time fragments and revised sections of *Under Milk Wood* were still being handed to the actors while they were applying their make-up. Some lines were not distributed until the actors were actually taking their places on stage. Yet, despite these last minute preparations, Brinnin described a spellbinding performance. "When the lights slowly faded and the night had swallowed up the last face and muffled the last voice in the village, there was an unexpected silence both on stage and off. The thousand spectators sat as if stunned, as if the slightest handclap might violate a spell. But within a few moments the lights went up and applause crescendoed and bravos were shouted by half the standing audience while the cast came back for curtain call after curtain call until, at the fifteenth of these, squat and boyish in his happily flustered modesty, Dylan stepped out alone."

Thomas continued to work in snatches on *Under Milk Wood* through the summer and early autumn until it was finally completed in October. It was the performance of this completed version on October 25, 1953 that Thomas was so happy to hear. After years he had finally produced the work he wanted.

Selections from
UNDER MILK WOOD

Although the small Welsh village and New York's sprawling metropolis may seem miles apart in makeup as well as distance, a close reading of *Under Milk Wood* shows a common thread of character, idiosyncracies, and human baseness which binds both settings equally.

New York was intimately involved in the final stages of the development of *Under Milk Wood.* The following selections have been excerpted from the play to accompany the present-day photographs of scenes Dylan Thomas visited and knew. The lines give added meaning to the photographs, and the photographs in turn complement the text in a special way.

Savor the lines from *Under Milk Wood* that follow. Let them roll off your tongue. And savor the New York sights which were part of Dylan Thomas' own life. For him they had meaning too.

FIRST VOICE *(Very softly)*

To begin at the beginning:

It is Spring, moonless night in the small town, starless and bible-black, the cobble-streets silent and the hunched, courters'-and-rabbits' wood limping invisible down to the sloeblack, slow, black, crowblack, fishingboat-bobbing sea.

Patchin Place in Greenwich Village

Hush, the babies are sleeping, the farmers, the fishers, the tradesmen and pensioners, cobbler, schoolteacher, postman and publican, the undertaker and the fancy women, drunkard, dressmaker, preacher, policeman, the webfoot cocklewomen and the tidy wives. Young girls lie bedded soft or glide in their dreams, with rings and trousseaux, bridesmaided by glowworms down the aisles of the organplaying wood. The boys are dreaming wicked or of the bucking ranches of the night and the jollyrodgered sea. And the anthracite statues of the horses sleep in the fields, and the cows in the byres, and the dogs in the wetnosed yards; and the cats nap in the slant corners or lope sly, streaking and needling, on the one cloud of the roofs.

You can hear the dew falling, and the hushed town breathing.

Minetta Tavern on Macdougal Street

Listen. It is night moving in the streets.

Hudson and West 11th Streets

Time passes. Listen. Time passes.

Come closer now.

Only you can hear the houses sleeping in the streets in the slow deep salt and silent black, bandaged night. Only you can see, in the blinded bedrooms, the combs and petticoats over the chairs, the jugs and basins, the glasses of teeth, Thou Shalt Not on the wall, and the yellowing dickybird-watching pictures of the dead. Only you can hear and see, behind the eyes of the sleepers, the movements and countries and mazes and colours and dismays and rainbows and tunes and wishes and flight and fall and despairs and big seas of their dreams.

From where you are, you can hear their dreams.

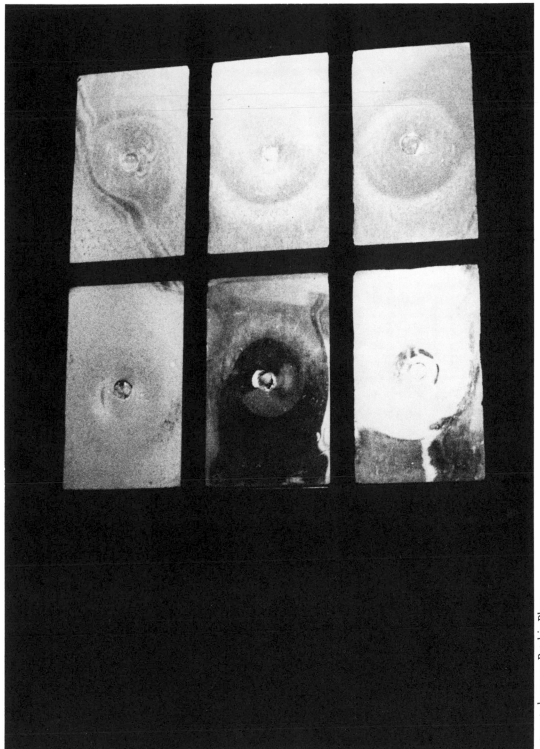

Doorway to house on Patchin Place

Gas lamp in Patchin Place

THIRD NEIGHBOUR

Black as a chimbley

FOURTH NEIGHBOUR

Ringing doorbells

THIRD NEIGHBOUR

Breaking windows

FOURTH NEIGHBOUR

Making mudpies

THIRD NEIGHBOUR

Stealing currants

FOURTH NEIGHBOUR

Chalking words

THIRD NEIGHBOUR

Saw him in the bushes

FOURTH NEIGHBOUR

Playing mwchins

LITTLE BOY

Give us a kiss, Matti Richards.

LITTLE GIRL

Give us a penny then.

MR. WALDO

I only got a halfpenny.

FIRST WOMAN

Lips is a penny.

The Grand Ticino Restaurant on Thompson Street

Now, in her iceberg-white, holily laundered crinoline nightgown, under virtuous polar sheets, in her spruced and scoured dust-defying bedroom in trig and trim Bay View, a house for paying guests at the top of the town, Mrs Ogmore-Pritchard, widow, twice, of Mr Ogmore, linoleum, retired, and Mr Pritchard, failed bookmaker, who maddened by besoming, swabbing and scrubbing, the voice of the vacuum-cleaner and the fume of polish, ironically swallowed disinfectant, fidgets in her rinsed sleep, wakes in a dream, and nudges in the ribs dead Mr Ogmore, dead Mr Pritchard, ghostly on either side.

Mr Ogmore!
Mr Pritchard!
It is time to inhale your balsam.

Hotel Chelsea on West 23rd Street

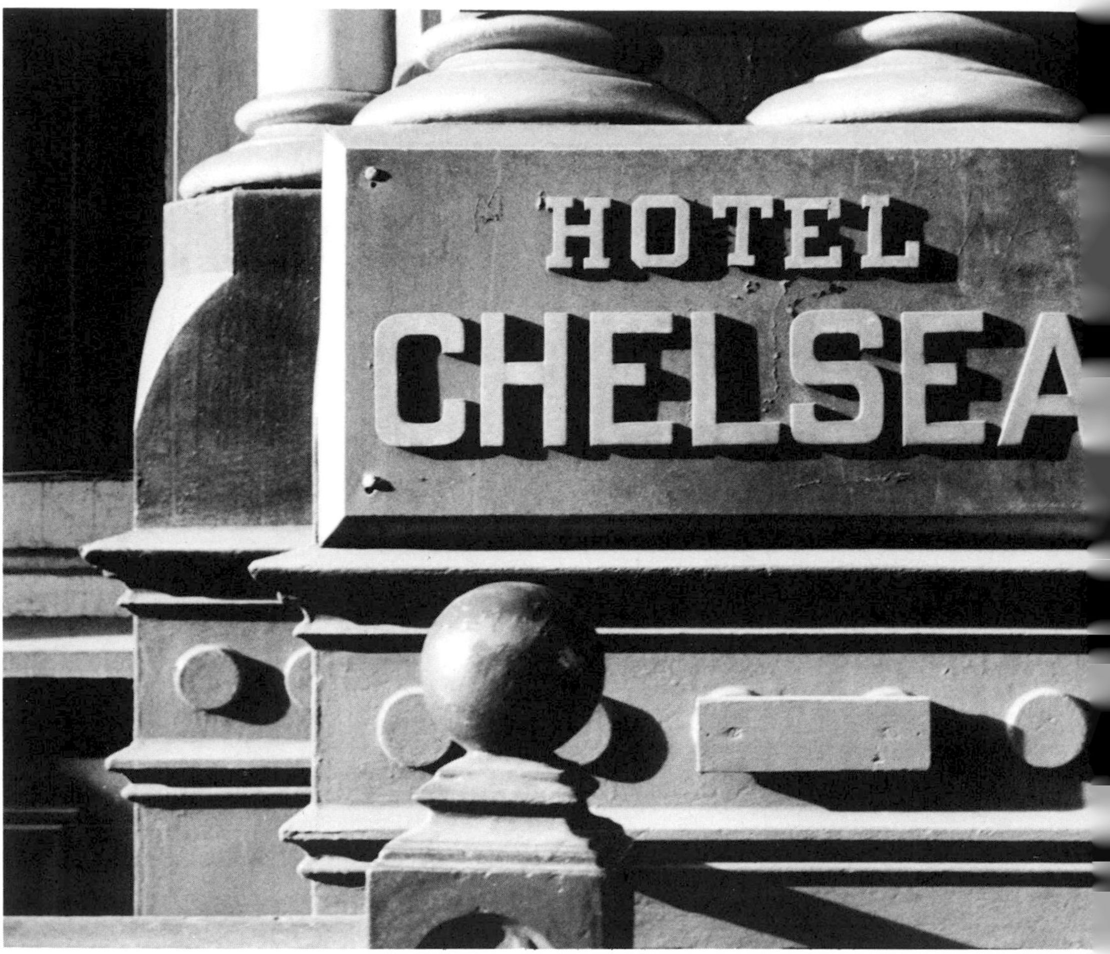

Sign at entrance to Hotel Chelsea

MRS OGMORE-PRITCHARD
And before you let the sun in, mind it wipes
its shoes.

At the sea-end of town, Mr and Mrs Floyd, the cocklers, are sleeping as quiet as death, side by wrinkled side, toothless, salt and brown, like two old kippers in a box.

Hotel Earle on Waverly Place

And high above, in Salt Lake Farm, Mr Utah Watkins counts, all night, the wife-faced sheep as they leap the fences on the hill, smiling and knitting and bleating just like Mrs Utah Watkins.

UTAH WATKINS (Yawning)

Thirty-four, thirty-five, thirty-six, forty-eight, eighty-nine . . .

MRS UTAH WATKINS (Bleating)

Knit one slip one
Knit two together
Pass the slipstitch over . . .

Cherry Owen, next door, lifts a tankard to his lips but nothing flows out of it. He shakes the tankard. It turns into a fish. He drinks the fish.

Glass cabinet at White Horse Tavern

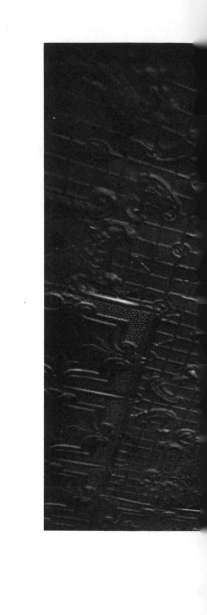

Pressed tin ceiling at the White Horse

A VOICE (Murmuring)
You'll be sorry for this in the morning.

Now behind the eyes and secrets of the dreamers in the streets rocked to sleep by the sea, see the

titbits and topsyturvies, bobs and buttontops, bags and bones, ash and rind and dandruff and nailparings, saliva and snowflakes and moulted feathers of dreams, the wrecks and sprats and shells and fishbones, whalejuice and moonshine and small salt fry dished up by the hidden sea.

Menu board at White Horse Tavern

Skylight at Hotel Chelsea

Time passes. Listen. Time passes. An owl flies home past Bethesda, to a chapel in an oak. And the dawn inches up.

Stand on this hill. This is Llareggub Hill, old as the hills, high, cool, and green, and from this small circle of stones, made not by druids but by Mrs Beynon's Billy, you can see all the town below you sleeping in the first of the dawn.

You can hear the love-sick woodpigeons mooning in bed. A dog barks in his sleep, farmyards away. The town ripples like a lake in the waking haze.

Balconies on front of Hotel Chelsea

REVEREND ELI JENKINS
A tiny dingle is Milk Wood
By Golden Grove 'neath Grongar,
But let me choose and oh! I should
Love all my life and longer

To stroll among our trees and stray
In Goosegog Lane, on Donkey Down,
And hear the Dewi sing all day,
And never, never leave the town.

Flute players in Washington Square

Back room at "The Horse"

Look at your complexion!
Oh, no, *you* look.
Needs a bit of make-up.
Needs a veil.
Oh, there's glamour!

Where you get that smile, Lil?
Never you mind, girl.
Nobody loves you.
That's what *you* think.

Staircase at Hotel Chelsea

MRS BEYNON (Loudly, from above)

Lily!

LILY SMALLS (Loudly)

Yes, mum.

MRS BEYNON

Where's my tea, girl?

LILY SMALLS

(Softly) Where d'you think? In the cat-box?
(Loudly) Coming up, mum.

MR PUGH

Here's your arsenic, dear.
And your weedkiller biscuit.
I've throttled your parakeet.
I've spat in the vases.
I've put cheese in the mouseholes.
Here's your . . .   *[Door creaks open]*
          . . . nice tea, dear.

MRS PUGH

Too much sugar.

MR PUGH

You haven't tasted it yet, dear.

MRS PUGH

Too much milk, then.

Ladies' restroom at White Horse Tavern

FIRST VOICE

Mary Ann Sailors, opening her bedroom window above the taproom and calling out to the heavens

MARY ANN SAILORS

I'm eighty-five years three months and a day!

MRS PUGH

I will say this for her, she never makes a
mistake.

POLLY GARTER
Oh, isn't life a terrible thing, thank God?

Now frying-pans spit, kettles and cats purr in the kitchen. The town smells of seaweed and breakfast all the way down from Bay View, where Mrs Ogmore-Pritchard, in smock and turban, big-besomed to engage the dust, picks at her starchless bread and sips lemon-rind tea, to Bottom Cottage, where Mr Waldo, in bowler and bib, gobbles his bubble-and-squeak and kippers and swigs from the saucebottle.

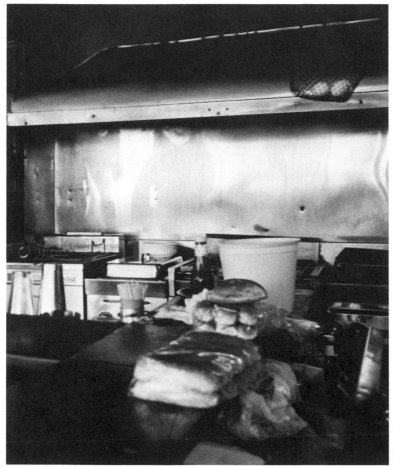

White Horse Tavern

MRS CHERRY OWEN

Remember last night? In you reeled, my boy, as drunk as a deacon with a big wet bucket and a fishfrail full of stout and you looked at me and you said, 'God has come home!' you said, and then over the bucket you went, sprawling and bawling, and the floor was all flagons and eels.

CHERRY OWEN

Was I wounded?

MRS CHERRY OWEN

And then you took off your trousers and you said, 'Does anybody want a fight!' Oh, you old baboon.

CHERRY OWEN

Give me a kiss.

MRS CHERRY OWEN

And then you sang 'Bread of Heaven,' tenor and bass.

CHERRY OWEN

I *always* sing 'Bread of Heaven.'

MRS CHERRY OWEN

And then you did a little dance on the table.

CHERRY OWEN

I did?

MRS CHERRY OWEN

Drop dead!

CHERRY OWEN

And then what did I do?

MRS CHERRY OWEN

Then you cried like a baby and said you were a poor drunk orphan with nowhere to go but the grave.

Hallway in Hotel Chelsea

Up the street, in the Sailors Arms, Sinbad
Sailors, grandson of Mary Ann Sailors, draws
a pint in the sunlit bar. The ship's clock in
the bar says half past eleven. Half past eleven
is opening time. The hands of the clock have
stayed still at half past eleven for fifty years.
It is always opening time in the Sailors Arms.

Mirror behind the bar at "The Horse"

And in the town, the shops squeak open. Mr Edwards, in butterfly-collar and straw-hat at the doorway of Manchester House, measures with his eye the dawdlers-by for striped flannel shirts and shrouds and flowery blouses, and bellows to himself in the darkness behind his eye.

Flatiron Building at 23rd Street and Broadway

All the women are out this morning, in the sun. You can tell it's Spring. There goes Mrs Cherry, you can tell her by her trotters, off she trots new as a daisy. Who's that talking by the pump? Mrs Floyd and Boyo, talking flatfish. What can you talk about flatfish? That's Mrs Dai Bread One, waltzing up the street like a jelly, every time she shakes it's slap slap slap. Who's that? Mrs Butcher Beynon with her pet black cat, it follows her everywhere, miaow and all. There goes Mrs Twenty-Three, important, the sun gets up and goes down in her dewlap, when she shuts her eyes, it's night. High heels now, in the morning too, Mrs Rose Cottage's eldest Mae, seventeen and never been kissed ho ho, going young and milking under my window to the field with the nannygoats, she reminds me all the way. Can't hear what the women are gabbing round the pump. Same as ever.

Strollers in Washington Square

Who's having a baby, who blacked whose
eye, seen Polly Garter giving her belly an
airing, there should be a law, seen Mrs
Beynon's new mauve jumper, it's her old grey
jumper dyed, who's dead, who's dying,
there's a lovely day, oh the cost of soapflakes!

There's the clip clop of horses on the sunhoneyed cobbles of the humming streets, hammering of horseshoes, gobble quack and cackle, tomtit twitter from the bird-ounced boughs, braying on Donkey Down. Bread is baking, pigs are grunting, chop goes the butcher, milk-churns bell, tills ring, sheep cough, dogs shout, saws sing. Oh, the Spring whinny and morning moo from the clog-dancing farms, the gulls' gab and rabble on the boat-bobbing river and sea and the cockles bubbling in the sand, scamper of sanderlings, curlew cry, crow caw, pigeon coo, clock strike, bull bellow, and the ragged gabble of the beargarden school as the women scratch and babble in Mrs Organ Morgan's general shop where everything is sold: custard, buckets, henna, rat-traps, shrimp-nets, sugar, stamps, confetti, paraffin, hatchets, whistles.

Waverly Place and the Hotel Earle

THIRD WOMAN

Seen Mrs Butcher Beynon?

SECOND WOMAN

she said Butcher Beynon put dogs in the mincer

FIRST WOMAN

go on, he's pulling her leg

West 11th Street near the White Horse

THIRD WOMAN

now don't you dare tell her that, there's a
dear

SECOND WOMAN

or she'll think he's trying to pull it off and
eat it.

FOURTH WOMAN

There's a nasty lot live here when you come
to think.

Stairwell at the Hotel Chelsea

SECOND WOMAN
And look at Ocky Milkman's wife that
nobody's ever seen

FIRST WOMAN
he keeps her in the cupboard with the
empties

Outside, the sun springs down on the rough
and tumbling town. It runs through the
hedges of Goosegog Lane, cuffing the birds
to sing. Spring whips green down Cockle

View of row houses from roof of Hotel Chelsea

Row, and the shells ring out. Llareggub this snip of a morning is wildfruit and warm, the streets, fields, sands and waters springing in the young sun.

And Willy Nilly, rumbling, jockeys out again
to the three-seated shack called the House of
Commons in the back where the hens weep,
and sees, in sudden Springshine,

herring gulls heckling down to the harbour
where the fishermen spit and prop the
morning up and eye the fishy sea smooth to
the sea's end as it lulls in blue. Green and
gold money, tobacco, tinned salmon, hats
with feathers, pots of fish-paste, warmth for
the winter-to-be, weave and leap in it rich
and slippery in the flash and shapes of fishes
through the cold sea-streets. But with blue
lazy eyes the fishermen gaze at that milkmaid
whispering water with no ruck or ripple as
though it blew great guns and serpents and
typhooned the town.

Too rough for fishing to-day.

And they thank God, and gob at a gull for luck, and moss-slow and silent make their way uphill, from the still still sea, towards the Sailors Arms

Sign over entrance to the White Horse

Johnnie Crack and Flossie Snail
Kept their baby in a milking pail
One would put it back and one would pull
   it out
And all it had to drink was ale and stout
For Johnnie Crack and Flossie Snail
Always used to say that stout and ale
Was *good* for a baby in a milking pail.

Beer sign in window of the White Horse Tavern

POLLY GARTER (Singing)

I loved a man whose name was Tom
He was strong as a bear and two yards long
I loved a man whose name was Dick
He was big as a barrel and three feet thick
And I loved a man whose name was Harry
Six feet tall and sweet as a cherry
But the one I loved best awake or asleep
Was little Willy Wee and he's six feet deep.

Table in front room of "The Horse"

MR WALDO
There goes the Reverend,

FIRST VOICE
says Mr Waldo at the smoked herring brown
window of the unwashed Sailors Arms,

MR WALDO
with his brolly and his odes. Fill 'em up,
Sinbad, I'm on the treacle to-day.

DOG TRAINING
HOUSEBREAKING A SPECIALTY
DESTRUCTIVENESS STOPPED
HAND AND VOICE SIGNALS
VICIOUSNESS TEMPERED
"MR. KINDNESS"   691-9084

CHEESEBURGER $1.30
HAMBURGER   1.
LIVERWURST   .8
FRENCH FRIES   .50
EGG   .25
COFFEE   .50
SODA   .5
FRANKS

Behind the bar at the White Horse

SECOND VOICE

The silent fishermen flush down their pints.

GIRL

Kiss me in Milk Wood Dicky
Or give me a penny quickly.

THIRD BOY

Gwennie Gwennie
I can't kiss you in Milk Wood.

GIRLS' VOICES

Gwennie ask him why.

GIRL

Why?

THIRD BOY

Because my mother says I mustn't.

GIRLS' VOICES

Cowardy cowardy custard
Give Gwennie a penny.

GIRL

Give me a penny.

THIRD BOY

I haven't got any.

Put him in the river
Up to his liver
Quick quick Dirty Dick
Beat him on the bum
With a rhubarb stick.
Aiee!
Hush!

Bicycle in front of YM-YWHA

Then his tormentors tussle and run to the Cockle Street sweet-shop, their pennies sticky as honey, to buy from Miss Myfanwy Price, who is cocky and neat as a puff-bosomed robin and her small round buttocks tight as ticks, gobstoppers big as wens that rainbow as you suck, brandyballs, winegums, hundreds and thousands, liquorice sweet as sick, nougat to tug and ribbon out like another red rubbery tongue, gum to glue in girls' curls, crimson coughdrops to spit blood, ice-cream cornets, dandelion-and-burdock, raspberry and cherryade, pop goes the weasel and the wind.

West 10th Street in Greenwich Village

FIRST VOICE

In the blind-drawn dark dining-room of School House, dusty and echoing as a dining-room in a vault, Mr and Mrs Pugh are silent over cold grey cottage pie. Mr Pugh reads, as he forks the shroud meat in, from *Lives of the Great Poisoners.* He has bound a plain brown-paper cover round the book. Slyly, between slow mouthfuls, he sidespies up at Mrs Pugh, poisons her with his eye, then goes on reading. He underlines certain passages and smiles in secret.

MRS PUGH

Persons with manners do not read at table,

says Mrs Pugh. She swallows a digestive tablet as big as a horse-pill, washing it down with clouded peasoup water. *(Pause)*

MRS PUGH

Some persons were brought up in pigsties.

MR PUGH

Pigs don't read at table, dear.

FIRST VOICE

Bitterly she flicks dust from the broken cruet. It settles on the pie in a thin gnat-rain.

MR PUGH

Pigs can't read, my dear.

MRS PUGH

I know one who can.

MR PUGH

You know best, dear,

FIRST VOICE

says Mr Pugh, and quick as a flash he ducks her in rat soup.

Lord Cut-Glass, in his kitchen full of time, squats down alone to a dogdish, marked Fido, of peppery fish-scraps and listens to the voices of his sixty-six clocks—(one for each year of his loony age)—and watches, with love, their black-and-white moony loudlipped faces tocking the earth away: slow clocks, quick clocks, pendulumed heart-knocks, china, alarm, grandfather, cuckoo; clocks shaped like Noah's whirring Ark, clocks that bicker in marble ships, clocks in the wombs of glass women, hourglass chimers, tu-wit-tu-woo clocks, clocks that pluck tunes, Vesuvius clocks all black bells and lava, Niagara clocks that cataract their ticks, old time-weeping clocks with ebony beards, clocks with no hands for ever drumming out time without ever knowing what time it is. His sixty-six singers are all set at different hours. Lord Cut-Glass lives in a house and a life at siege. Any minute or dark day now, the unknown enemy will loot and savage downhill, but they will not catch him napping. Sixty-six different times in his fish-slimy kitchen ping, strike, tick, chime, and tock.

Clock tower of Jefferson Market Courthouse

The arch in Washington Square

The sunny slow lulling afternoon yawns and moons through the dozy town. The sea lolls, laps and idles in, with fishes sleeping in its lap. The meadows still as Sunday, the shut-eye tasselled bulls, the goat-and-daisy dingles, nap happy and lazy. The dumb duck-ponds snooze. Clouds sag and pillow on Llareggub Hill.

Captain Cat, at his window thrown wide to the sun and the clippered seas he sailed long ago when his eyes were blue and bright, slumbers and voyages; earringed and rolling, I Love You Rosie Probert tatooed on his belly, he brawls with broken bottles in the fug and babel of the dark dock bars, roves with a herd of short and good time cows in every naughty port and twines and souses with the drowned and blowzy-breasted dead. He weeps as he sleeps and sails.

Third floor window on West 11th Street

MAE ROSE COTTAGE (Lazily)

He loves me
He loves me not
He loves me
He loves me not
He *loves* me!—the dirty old fool.

Julius' bar on West 10th Street

The bar rail at the White Horse

REVEREND ELI JENKINS

Poor Dad,

SECOND VOICE

grieves the Reverend Eli,

REVEREND ELI JENKINS

to die of drink and agriculture.

Farmer Watkins in Salt Lake Farm hates his cattle on the hill as he ho's them in to milking.

Damn you, you damned dairies!

A cow kisses him.

Bite her to death!

he shouts to his deaf dog who smiles and licks his hands.

Gore him, sit on him, Daisy!

he bawls to the cow who barbed him with her
tongue, and she moos gentle words as he
raves and dances among his summerbreathed
slaves walking delicately to the farm. The
coming of the end of the Spring day is
already reflected in the lakes of their great
eyes.

Roof of Hotel Chelsea

Now the town is dusk. Each cobble, donkey, goose and gooseberry street is a thoroughfare of dusk; and dusk and ceremonial dust, and night's first darkening snow, and the sleep of birds, drift under and through the live dusk of this place of love. Llareggub is the capital of dusk.

Front windows of "The Horse"

And every evening at sun-down
I ask a blessing on the town,
For whether we last the night or no
I'm sure is always touch-and-go.

We are not wholly bad or good
Who live our lives under Milk Wood,
And Thou, I know, wilt be the first
To see our best side, not our worst.

O let us see another day!
Bless us this night, I pray,
And to the sun we all will bow
And say, good-bye—but just for now!

10th Street and Waverly Place

And Cherry Owen, sober as Sunday as he is
every day of the week, goes off happy as
Saturday to get drunk as a deacon as he does
every night.

I always say she's got two husbands,

says Cherry Owen,

one drunk and one sober.

And Mrs Cherry simply says

And aren't I a lucky woman? Because I love
them both.

White Horse Tavern at night

SINBAD

Evening, Cherry.

CHERRY OWEN

Evening, Sinbad.

SINBAD

What'll you have?

CHERRY OWEN

Too much.

Clean glasses on the bar at the White Horse

Dusk is drowned for ever until to-morrow. It is all at once night now. The windy town is a hill of windows, and from the larrupped waves the lights of the lamps in the windows call back the day and the dead that have run away to sea. All over the calling dark, babies and old men are bribed and lullabied to sleep.

St. Vincent's Hospital

The drinkers in the Sailors Arms drink to the failure of the dance.

Down with the waltzing and the skipping.

Dancing isn't natural,

righteously says Cherry Owen who has just downed seventeen pints of flat, warm, thin, Welsh, bitter beer.

Minetta Tavern on Macdougal Street

And all the fare I could afford
Was parsnip gin and watercress.
I did not need a knife and fork
Or a bib up to my chin
To dine on a dish of watercress
And a jug of parsnip gin.
Did you ever hear a growing boy
To live so cruel cheap
On grub that has no flesh and bones
And liquor that makes you weep?

Portrait of Dylan Thomas at the White Horse Tavern

The thin night darkens. A breeze from the creased water sighs the streets

Empty chair at "The Horse"

Text researched, written, photographed and designed by
Tryntje Van Ness Seymour

Photographs on the cover and page 15 by Bunny Adler, courtesy of Rollie
McKenna

Cover designed by Victor A. Curran

Quotations from *Under Milk Wood* and display composed in phototype
Garamond by Catherine Graphics, Inc., New York City

Introduction, walking map, copyright page and colophon composed in phototype
Garamond by the Monotype Composition Company, Baltimore, Maryland

Printed on 80-pound Glatfelter Offset and bound in paper by the John D. Lucas
Printing Company, Baltimore, Maryland